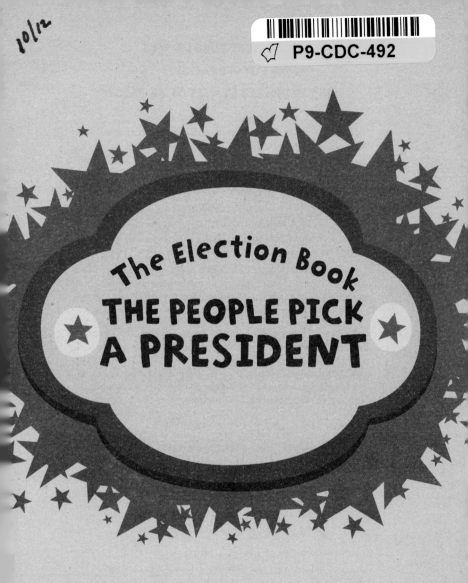

The Election Book
THE PEOPLE PICK A PRESIDENT

SCHOLASTIC INC.

NEW YORK · TORONTO · LONDON · AUCKLAND
SYDNEY · MEXICO CITY · NEW DELHI · HONG KONG

FOR THE FUTURE VOTERS
—AND FUTURE PRESIDENTS—
OF THE UNITED STATES OF AMERICA

Acknowledgments:
Special thanks to Lee Kravitz for his support and encourage-
ment when I was writing this book, to Carol Drisko and Steven
Manning for sharing their expertise, and to the people at the
Congressional Quarterly and the Federal Election Commission
for their patient and prompt answers to all my questions.

....

All presidential portraits courtesy of
the White House Historical Association

....

ISBN 978-0-545-45783-5

Text by Tamara Henneman
Updated text for 2004, 2008, and 2012 editions
by Carolyn Jackson
cover art © 2012 by Roman Shcherbakov/iStock
Book design by Kay Petronio

10 9 8 7 6 5 4 3 2 1   12 13 14 15 16

Printed in the U.S.A.   40
This updated edition first printing, April 2012

CONTENTS

PREFACE

Every four years, Americans elect a president. The election is the top story in the media for more than a year before the election. Yet most people don't know very much about how the election really works.

Since we have a government of the people, by the people, and for the people, it's important that people—including people like you—know what goes on in an election year. *The Election Book* tells the story. When you read it, you'll know more about choosing a president than most Americans. And although it may be a few years before you can vote, you'll be able to follow the news and understand what is happening today.

GOVERNMENT BY THE VOTERS

The United States is a democracy. This means the people have the power to decide who runs the government. Every four years Americans get to choose a president, the country's single most powerful and important leader.

During an election year, all eyes are on the presidential candidates. The candidates are in the headlines and on the evening news. Everywhere you turn, you see a candidate's face on a poster, or name on a bumper sticker.

But the real power during the election is with the people. Each candidate, whether giving a speech, touring a factory, or appearing on television, has just one goal in an election year. That is to get the votes of the people.

The U.S. presidential election is probably the longest and the toughest race in the world to win. And the winner ends up with one of the toughest but most important jobs in the world. Only a few Americans get into the race for president, but millions of Americans take part in choosing the winner.

THE NATION'S TOP LEADER

When the people choose a president, they are choosing the person who will have the most powerful, prestigious, and difficult job in the country, maybe even in the world. From the Oval Office in the White House, the president carries out a lot of responsibilities.

THE PRESIDENT'S MANY JOBS

The president is the chief executive and heads the executive branch of the U.S. government. The president suggests laws to Congress that shape nearly every aspect of our society, from business to education, from housing to health care. He or she is "boss" to the millions of government workers who see that laws are carried out.

As chief of state, the president is the ultimate leader of the American people. He or she must inspire and lead the country through both good times and bad times.

The president is America's top diplomat, meeting with foreign leaders and deciding what the country's foreign policy will be.

Also commander-in-chief, the president is in charge of all U.S. armed forces—the Army, Navy, Air Force, and Marines.

THE PRESIDENT'S TOP ADVISORS

To do each of these jobs, the president needs help from many experts in different fields, including international politics, education, economics, agriculture, transportation, and more. The president chooses fifteen experts to be in the cabinet, his or her top group of advisors. These are people who have the president's deepest trust and highest respect.

When choosing a candidate for president, voters often consider who might be appointed to the cabinet. They want to choose someone who is capable of doing all of the president's jobs well, and someone who will get the best advice.

George Washington's first cabinet meeting included secretaries of state, war (today called defense), and treasury. Later, he added the secretary of the navy and the attorney general, who was and is the nation's chief prosecutor. As the nation grew and government became more complicated, the cabinet was enlarged. In 2011, the cabinet of Barack Obama had fifteen members in addition to Vice President Joseph Biden. This included Secretary of State Hillary Clinton, who had been Obama's chief Democratic rival during his presidential race. Women have served in the cabinet since 1933, when President Franklin Roosevelt named

Frances Perkins as Secretary of Labor. But all the members were white until 1966, when President Lyndon B. Johnson named African American Robert Weaver the Secretary of Housing and Urban Development.

WHO CAN BE PRESIDENT?

The Written Rules

The 2008 election made real history when Barack Obama became the first African American president. The Republican candidates who might challenge him in 2012 include Newt Gingrich, Mitt Romney, Rick Santorum, and Ron Paul.

WHO IS ELIGIBLE FOR THE JOB?

The Constitution, which is the set of rules defining our government, requires that the president must

- be at least 35 years old
- have lived in the United States for 14 years
- be a "natural-born citizen" of the United States. (Basically, that means you have to be born in the United States. Some people say you're also a "natural-born citizen" if at least one of your parents is a U.S. citizen, but your mother happened to be out of the country when you were born. No one born under these circumstances has ever tried to run for president. When someone does, the government will have to decide whether that person is a "natural-born citizen.")

HOW DOES A PERSON GET THE JOB?

The Constitution also describes some surprising things about how a person can get the job of president. The most important day in an election year is the first Tuesday after the first Monday in November. That is Election Day, the day Americans vote for president. But what most people don't know, or what they forget, is that their votes do not directly elect the president. The Constitution says the Electoral College must choose the president.

WHO REALLY ELECTS THE PRESIDENT?

When the Constitution was written, the founders worried that would-be tyrants would appeal to uneducated voters. To guard against this, they decided that the people would not directly elect the president and senators. In 1913, the Constitution was amended so that voters, not state legislatures, elected senators. However, the Constitution was left unchanged about the election of the president. It still says that a group of electors from each state, not the voters, select the president. Originally, these electors were educated men who were expected to use their independent judgment. Today, electors are expected to cast their ballots for the candidate who receives the most votes in their state on Election Day. Usually, that's what they do, but they are not legally bound in every state. Together, the electors are called the Electoral College. It is not a school, but a virtual group that meets in mid-December after a presidential election to cast its votes.

HOW THE ELECTORAL COLLEGE WORKS

If you look at the ballot in a presidential election, you will see that electors are listed for each candidate. Technically, the voter selects the electors, not the presidential or vice presidential candidate. Many people have urged that the Constitution be amended so that the people directly elect the president. This is because it is possible for a candidate to receive the most popular votes and still lose in the Electoral College. This has happened four times in the nation's history. The last time was in 2000.

To see a chart showing the results of every presidential election, turn to page 91.

GOVERNORS

LAWYERS

SENATORS

WHO CAN BE PRESIDENT?

The Unwritten Rules

Most of the qualities and qualifications that a candidate for president needs are not written in the laws of the land. Neither are many of the steps Americans take in choosing their top leader. There are many "unwritten" rules about who can become president and how they get the job. The American people decide what those rules are and change them slightly each time they elect a president.

Since the Constitution was written, the standards by which Americans judge their presidential candidates have evolved and changed. So have the methods used to choose a person for the job. The serious contenders for the presidency know what the people expect from a leader, and they set out to prove they can do the job.

EXPERIENCE

Candidates need the right kind of experience before people will consider them seriously as a potential president. People from many different professions go on to become presidents, but every president has had experience in government or experience leading a large organization before getting the country's top job.

Since the 1960s, many candidates for president have been governors and/or U.S. senators. Twenty-six presidents have been lawyers. Several—among them Washington, Jackson, Grant, and Eisenhower—have been military leaders. Others have been farmers, teachers, and businessmen. A former actor, Ronald Reagan, became one of our most popular presidents.

COURAGE AND CONVICTION

A candidate for president must be convinced, beyond a doubt, that he or she is the best person for the job. To be president, a person needs powerful ideas about what he or she can do for the country and has to convince people to support these ideas.

During the campaign season, the whole country will judge both the candidates and their ideas. The country watches everything the candidates do. Journalists report on and question every decision candidates make during the campaign, and nearly every decision in their lives previous to the campaign. A candidate has to have courage to face the people's judgment during the campaign and the courage to lead them if he or she is elected.

ENERGY AND SPIRIT

The campaign for president is long and grueling. Candidates travel all over the United States during the campaign, sometimes visiting five or more states a day. Most candidates for president are spouses and parents, too. They have to be away from their families and friends for weeks at a time. Even if candidates are exhausted and miss their families, they must keep their spirits up and show their best side.

Some people say the American election process is too long and too exhausting for the candidates. Others say that it is a good test to see if a person can withstand the rigors of being president.

MONEY

Presidential candidates spend more money running for office with every election. In 2008, the candidates spent a combined $5.3 billion. The cost of the 2012 election is expected to reach $8 billion.

PARTY FAVORITES

Since 1852, no candidate has won a presidential election without first being nominated by the Democratic Party or the Republican Party. But this was not always true. Early U.S. political parties included the Democratic-Republicans, the

Federalists, and the Whigs.

Political leaders began forming the parties more than 100 years ago as a way of getting many people to support one person for president. Today, the two parties dominate our system of government. Each party has its own system for nominating and supporting a candidate for president. Independent candidates who are not affiliated with any party can also run for office.

During many election years, new parties form to back a presidential candidate. One of the alternate or "third" parties can affect the election by drawing support away from the main parties, but the Democrats and the Republicans have the most power when it comes to electing a president.

Although the Constitution does not mention political parties, we have had national parties since 1800. Today, two parties—

the Republicans and the Democrats—dominate our system of government. Each party has its own system for nominating and supporting its candidates. One of the unofficial roles of a president has been to head the party that elected him.

There are other, smaller political parties, too. These "third" parties often form over issues that are "hot buttons." Among the ideas that have made their way into politics via small parties are the eight-hour workday, the direct election of senators, and the practice of recall and referendum in state elections.

Former presidents Martin Van Buren, Millard Fillmore, and Theodore Roosevelt tried to make their way back into the White House through third parties, but they failed.

Today, there are many minor parties. Among the most popular "third" parties are the Green Party, which supports environmental causes and independence from corporations; the Libertarian Party, which supports lower taxes and non-interference in foreign policy; and the Socialist Workers Party, which supports trade unions.

Ralph Nader is perhaps the best-known and most successful third-party candidate. He has run for president five times since 1992. In 2000, running for the Green Party, he got almost 3 million popular votes.

PARTY POWER

Political parties are an important link between the voters and the candidates. They get many people involved in choosing candidates for president. They also organize people to support candidates, and help clarify the choice people have to make on Election Day.

Most candidates for president begin their political careers by working for one of the two main parties. They often campaign for other candidates before running for office themselves.

DEMOCRAT OR REPUBLICAN?

Most voters call themselves Democrats or Republicans. Even when they are independent, they usually vote for candidates from a major party in the November election. Sometimes we call them "swing voters" because they move from one party to another.

Today, most elected officials—from school-board members to members of Congress—are political party members, usually Democratic or Republican. Every four years, they may take part in their party's convention, where they agree on a set of goals called a platform.

The Democratic Party has been around since 1828. During the presidencies of John F. Kennedy and Lyndon B. Johnson, the party supported civil rights, labor unions, and Medicare. Later Democratic presidents Jimmy Carter and Bill Clinton were considered more moderate than Kennedy and Johnson.

The Republican Party has been around since 1854, and calls itself the Grand Old Party, or GOP. Abraham Lincoln was its first successful presidential candidate, in 1861. Although the GOP is usually a friend of business, Republican President Theodore "Teddy" Roosevelt was a progressive reformer of big business at the beginning of the twentieth century. President Ronald Reagan, who served from 1981 to 1989, is credited as a defender of conservative politics.

In 2012, near the end of Barack Obama's

first term, Republicans and Democrats disagreed about many issues, including whether tax cuts passed in the George W. Bush administration should end and whether the Obama health care plan of 2010 was constitutional.

PARTY MASCOTS

Both parties have mascots, and you will see a lot of them during an election year. The Democrats have the donkey, and the Republicans have the elephant. Strangely enough, both symbols were first used to make fun of the parties, but party leaders managed to turn this to their own advantage.

Andrew Jackson started the Democratic Party in 1828 when he was running for president. Jackson's political foes said he was as stubborn and foolish as a mule. Jackson shrugged off the name-calling and began using drawings of donkeys on his campaign posters. He went on to win the election! Today, you still find the donkey on Democratic campaign posters, buttons, and bumper stickers.

A political cartoonist in the 1870s began using the elephant to stand for the Republicans, probably because the party was then the largest in the country. The reference was not a compliment, however. The cartoon showed the elephant getting scared off by a donkey in a lion costume! Nevertheless, some people in the party must have liked the image. The elephant became a symbol of the party and now marches across the posters, buttons, and other campaign paraphernalia of the Republicans.

THE PICK OF THE PARTIES

A candidate's first goal is to win the

nomination for president from one of the major political parties. To do this, he or she has to win the support of party leaders and voters in every state, one state at a time.

Early in an election year, the major political parties in each state hold either an election called a "primary" or a meeting called a "caucus." The primaries and caucuses let party leaders know who the people support for president. They also determine who will be sent to the party's national convention in the summer. These representatives are called delegates. At the convention, they will vote to choose the party's official nominee for president.

PRIMARIES

A primary is a statewide election open to all members of the major political parties. Some states also have "open primaries" that people can vote in even if they are not a member of either political party. In most states, Republicans and Democrats have their primary elections on the same day. There can be many candidates running for each party's nomination. A voter must pick one candidate from *either* the Republican Party or the Democratic Party. They cannot vote in both primaries.

Although voters usually name a presidential candidate, what they are really doing is choosing delegates to go to the convention. Based on the primary vote totals, party leaders select delegates for the convention. The delegates are expected to represent the wishes expressed by the people's vote in the primary. In some states, people actually vote for the delegates instead of the presidential candidates.

CAUCUSES

Caucus meetings are like mini-elections in which only active party members can vote. Every state is divided into voting districts and precincts. Caucuses are meetings of all the active party members in a district or precinct. The party members vote for delegates to represent them at the convention, either knowing which candidate a delegate is likely to support or simply trusting in that delegate's judgment.

The state-by-state schedule for primaries and caucuses usually begins in January of an election year. Each week until June, a few states have their primaries or caucuses. During these six months, candidates rush from state to state, campaigning to win both the people's support and the support of the delegates who will attend the national conventions.

DECIDING TO RUN

Potential candidates think long and hard before deciding to run for president. They must consider everything described to you so far. Can they expect support from people in their political party *and* from the American voters? Can they raise enough money? Do they have faith and confidence in themselves and in their views on this country? Are they and their families ready to enter the longest, hardest election race in the world?

Years before the election, potential candidates may begin to "test the waters" to see if they have a chance at becoming president. They talk with other powerful people in their political party. They let it be known that they are interested in running for president and try to build support from within the party.

Potential candidates also travel around the country, meeting people, giving speeches, and raising money for a campaign. It is important to see how people

react to their ideas. They also want people to begin thinking about them as presidential material.

As the election year draws near, candidates begin to declare officially that they are running for president. Usually a candidate calls a press conference. In front of television cameras and news reporters, the candidate tells Americans, "I want to be your next president." If the current president wants to be reelected, a press conference is held to announce the decision.

From this point on, candidates are no longer "testing the waters." They are in the race.

THE CAMPAIGN TEAM

Candidates for president put together a team of people to help them run for office. A candidate hires a campaign manager to oversee every part of the campaign. Schedulers decide where and when candidates will meet the voters. "Advance people" make sure a candidate's supporters are on hand at each scheduled campaign stop. Press secretaries make sure the news reporters show up. Pollsters survey Americans to see how the candidate is doing. In an election year, hundreds of people have full-time jobs helping the candidates.

A president seeking reelection puts together a campaign team, too. A president has many advantages over other candidates in the race. The president is already familiar to Americans. Whenever the president does something even just a little bit interesting, it's on the news. But running for office from the White House is also very demanding. Often there are arguments and tensions between the campaign team and the regular advisors. They both want the president's time.

7

THE LONG CAMPAIGN

Usually, campaigning begins months—or even years—before the first primary. Candidates raise money, meet with potential supporters, and appear on television whenever possible.

THE CASH

Almost from the second a person begins thinking about the presidency, money is an issue. Where will it come from? Individual donors, special-interest groups, corporations, and even the government itself are possible sources. Each, however, comes with its own limitations.

Candidates are eager to raise money, and many people are eager to influence them. Campaign reformers try to measure the influence of money by tracking where it comes from and how it is spent. They believe that unidentified donations are a threat to democracy, because voters cannot judge the interests of the donors. In 1971, Congress passed the first Federal Election Campaign Act to keep track of federal contributions. Although the act was amended twice, candidates and contributors found ways to pump ever-increasing and unidentified dollars into campaigns.

In 2002, Congress passed the Bipartisan Campaign Reform Act, which is sometimes referred to by the names of its sponsors, Senators John McCain and Russell Feingold. The act banned "soft" money—contributions to political parties from corporations, labor unions, and wealthy individuals that parties could use any way they wanted.

The reform act set limits on how much a person could donate to a federal candidate's campaign in "hard" money, but allowed those amounts to be adjusted for inflation. In 2012, the limit per person for each election (primary or general) is $2,500, but a contributor could give a total of $117,000 to many different campaigns.

The McCain-Feingold Act banned contributions by people too young to vote, but that was later overturned by the courts. Today, you can donate to your favorite candidate.

In the 2000 election, only twelve percent of eligible voters contributed any money. But at least fifty donors gave $1 million or more in "soft" money. In 2004, that loophole was closed. Some organizations took up the slack and made sizable "soft" money donations. They did not work for candidates directly, but voters quickly figured out which side they were on and donated money to them accordingly. Although reformers asked Congress to make these organizations illegal in 2008, it did not.

Taxpayers raise money for public elections by checking off a dollar donation when they file their income taxes. If candidates want to use these funds, they have to agree to a limit on spending.

The Obama campaign rejected these funds in 2012. This decision was most likely based on the success of Obama's first presidential fundraising efforts. In

2008, the Obama campaign raised over half a billion dollars, $500 million of which was given via Internet donors, and $6 million from increments of $100 or less. Because it was easy to contribute in small amounts, Obama's initiative sparked a new era of digital fundraising, which allowed for a wider range of contributors.

In November 2011, a year before the presidential election, President Obama had raised $86.2 million for his re-election campaign. That was more than the $80.9 million combined total the eight leading Republican candidates reported. Republican donations are expected to increase once a candidate is selected.

MEETING PEOPLE

Candidates travel from state to state, giving speeches and meeting people. They go to schools, shopping malls, factories, farms, and town hangouts like bowling alleys and cafés. They try to tell as many people as they can about how they would make the country better if they were elected president. During the primaries, Democrats are running against Democrats and Republicans against Republicans. So each candidate tries to convince voters that he or she is the party's best hope for beating the other party.

MAINSTREAM MEDIA

No matter how much they travel, candidates can't meet everyone. So, they spend a lot of time trying to get television cameras and news photographers to cover their activities. They spend millions of dollars on television commercials and newspaper and online ads to get their message across to voters.

For many years, most people got their

news from network television—NBC, CBS, and ABC. But beginning in the 1980s, cable television began to gain an audience. By 1985, sixty-eight percent of American homes had cable service. Many people liked the raw energy of CNN or the conservative slant of Fox News. And lots of young people tuned in to MTV. These new channels gave candidates access to reach particular groups of voters.

Although the Internet began to draw some of television's audience by the 1990s, people still turned to television for candidate debates and election results. By the twenty-first century, they could watch television on their computers.

Radio, which nearly died in the fifties, enjoyed a comeback in the 1990s. Producers discovered that outrageous talk show hosts drew large audiences. One of the most popular was Rush Limbaugh, who in the mid-nineties gained a following for promoting conservative ideas and criticizing liberals. Conservative talk show hosts were so powerful that liberals launched their own radio network, Air America, to promote their agenda in this increasingly popular medium.

Newspapers, the oldest of the mainstream media, are not as popular as they once were. The habit of reading a daily newspaper started falling after World War II, when people started watching television. Today, only fifty-four percent of U.S. adults are daily readers. Still, papers like the *New York Times* and *USA Today* have readers across the nation. The best place to learn about who is running for state and city offices may be your local newspaper.

THE INTERNET

The Internet is the first technology to change politics since television became widespread in the 1950s. Commercial providers entered a field that had once belonged to government and scientists in the later eighties and early nineties. And the influence of what we now call telecommunications keeps growing, as service speeds up and users find new ways to reach people.

In 2004, politicians began to reach out to voters though their Web sites and e-mail. By 2008, the Internet was a major player, helping candidates raise money and as a vehicle for campaign messages and news that reached beyond the mainstream media. Web sites by candidates and partisans of every kind competed for attention, and newspapers and magazines developed their own sites. Democrats Barack Obama and John Edwards used the Web to attract young voters. Ron Paul, who ran in Republican primaries, set a record when he raised $1 million on the Internet in a single day. Ordinary citizens posted short videos through YouTube, and the most compelling went "viral" to thousands of viewers.

Soon, people were connecting to the Internet not only by their desktop and laptop computers but with new smart phones and electronic tablets. Social media, such as Facebook, helped people and organizations stay connected to a broad web of friends. Twitter made it possible to connect with brief, 140-character messages to their followers through tweets. No doubt they will be important in the 2012 election.

DEBATES

Candidates usually want to participate in debates with other candidates on television. These debates give voters the chance to learn what candidates think about the issues and how they act under pressure. During the primaries, the Republican candidates debate one another, and the Democrats do, too. Then, after the nominees are chosen, the leading candidates debate each other. In 2008, both Republicans and Democrats had large fields of candidates and many primary debates among them.

OPINION POLLS

Researchers have been asking people questions about how they vote since the 1930s. Candidates use them to figure out where they stand in the race and to identify people who are likely to vote for them. Candidates may also use polls to find out how voters feel on certain issues. Are they doing well economically? Should the government get more involved in health care? Which issues concern them most? But polls only measure one moment in time—in modern campaigns, things can change quickly.

THE FIELD NARROWS

If a party has a first-term president in the White House, it rarely has to find another candidate. Time, energy, and money can be spent building an organization for the general election. But if a president is serving a second term—the Constitution allows only two—the party must look for another candidate. Sometimes, it looks no further than the vice president. But in 2008, Vice President Dick Cheney had no interest in running. Twelve candidates ran serious campaigns for the Republican nomination. Eventually, Senator John McCain was the last man standing.

The race for president is grueling. Candidates must travel to many states, as they hold their primary elections or caucuses. Each party has its own rules for selecting a nominee, and candidates must strategize about the best way to gather the most delegates. The Democratic Party has two kinds of delegates, those chosen by election or caucus in each state, and "superdelegates" chosen because of their role in party politics. They usually divide their delegates in each state proportionally according to how many votes they received. The Republicans give all their delegates to the winner in each state.

For the 2008 election, the Democrats said that no state could have a primary before the Iowa caucus in February. But Michigan and Florida held their primaries in January, and later, the party had to decide if it would honor the results.

Democrats had a field of ten candidates. Eventually, the race came down to two unusual front-runners—Senator Hillary Clinton and Senator Barack Obama. The party had never nominated a woman or an African American. Because of this, the 2008 election was particularly historic.

PARTY CONVENTIONS

The Republican and Democratic parties each have a rowdy summertime meeting called a "convention." This is where their final choice for president is made. By the time of the convention, there are usually only two or three candidates left in the race for each party's nomination.

Often, one of those candidates is the clear front-runner for the nomination and has the support of plenty of delegates.

At convention time, all the delegates chosen in primaries and caucuses, and the powerful leaders from each party, gather. Republicans chose Tampa, Florida, for their 2012 convention, scheduled for the week of August 27. The site is the St. Petersburg Times Forum. Democrats scheduled their convention for the week of September 3 in Charlotte, North Carolina, the first time that state has hosted a national political convention.

Party members do three important jobs at the conventions: decide on a party platform, nominate a president, and nominate a vice president. It sounds like very official business, and it is.

Conventions are a time for political party members to meet and celebrate, and to show the whole country how spirited, enthusiastic, and confident they are.

Conventions last about three days. They open with a round of rousing speeches. Officials from the host city and state give welcoming speeches. Top party officials also speak. Then, a party leader gives the keynote address. This is an especially important speech. It dramatically sets forth the themes the party wants to stress and helps set the tone of the whole convention. As with all major events of the convention, planners try to schedule the keynote address during prime time for the television networks. That's usually around 8 P.M. Eastern Time. All the major networks broadcast the speech live.

THE PLATFORM

The first piece of major business is to adopt a platform. This is a statement of the party's goals and principles. A committee brings a draft of the platform to the convention, and "planks" or ideas are added or changed, until, finally, a majority of delegates vote to accept the platform.

CHOOSING THE CANDIDATE

Next, the convention moves on to the moment everyone has been waiting for: picking the nominee for president of the United States. Delegates from each state dress in red, white, and blue, wear funny hats, and wave banners and posters for the candidate they support.

Candidates are officially nominated by prominent party members, to the resounding cheers of their supporters. Then, state by state, each bank of delegates is called upon. With a flourish, one delegate will stand and announce the vote of that state's delegates, stating how many delegate votes go to each candidate who is up for nomination. In the first round of voting, the delegates are expected to vote for the candidate they had pledged to support during the party's primaries and caucuses. However, each party also sends delegates to the convention who are officially "uncommitted." They can vote for whomever they wish.

If one candidate gets a majority—or more than half—of the votes, then that candidate is the party's choice. If no candidate gets at least half of the votes, nominations are taken again. This is called a "brokered" convention. A candidate's supporters double their efforts to gain support before a second round of state-by-state balloting. If a candidate still does not get a majority of votes, another round of nominating and balloting is held. This will go on until one candidate wins a majority of the delegate votes and becomes the party's nominee for president.

After the first round of balloting, delegates are no longer bound to vote for the candidate they were pledged to in their state's primary or caucus. They can vote for whomever they think is the best candidate. Party leaders may choose to nominate someone who did not even run in the primaries or caucuses.

CHOOSING THE VICE PRESIDENT

Before any balloting takes place, candidates for the presidency usually announce who they want to run with them for the office of vice president. After the delegates choose a presidential nominee, they vote for the vice president, but balloting this time around is really just a formality. Everyone assumes that the delegates will vote for the candidate the presidential nominee wants as a running mate.

Choosing a vice president is often an opportunity for a presidential candidate to bridge gaps and mend fences with people in the party who do not enthusiastically support him or her. In 1980, Ronald Reagan and George H. W. Bush both ran for the Republican nomination for president. They waged an intense fight against each other that made many in the party angry. By asking Mr. Bush to be his running mate, the front-runner Ronald Reagan reunited his party.

HOOPLA TO THE LAST

In closing the convention, the candidates for the top two offices in the land give acceptance speeches. Again, convention planners make every effort to schedule the speeches during prime-time television viewing hours, so that as many Americans as possible will see the candidates. The delegates and other people at the convention keep cheering, waving banners, and throwing confetti until the end. They want to show the country how excited they are to get their candidate into office!

THE BIG SHOW

When the political conventions are over, both major parties have their candidates. There may be a break in the campaigning until after Labor Day.

This is not necessarily a calm period for the candidates and their parties.

There is a lot of work to be done. If the fight for the nomination has been a bitter one, the candidate tries to reunite his or her party for the big push ahead. There is poll-taking to find out what the voters are thinking. There are meetings with consultants and strategists to refine and polish the candidate's message and plan the campaign. What are the candidate's strengths? What are the opponent's weaknesses? What is the best way to show off both to the voters? What will the campaign slogans be?

MONEY

During the general election campaign, the federal government gives the Democratic and Republican candidates an equal amount of money to spend. (Independents and third-party candidates are on their own.) If the candidates accept this public funding, they must agree not to raise money from most private sources. For that reason, candidates who are very good at fund-raising may choose not to participate. In 2008, Republican nominee John McCain accepted more than $84 million in federal funds, while Democrat Barack Obama opted out of the program.

THE TWO-PERSON RACE

After Labor Day, campaigning begins again. The candidates resume their hectic travel schedules, again trying to meet as many voters as possible. This time around, candidates spend most of their time in the big states, where most of the voters are, and in states where the contest might be a close one. The big states have the most votes in the Electoral College. The candidates are trying to rack up enough electoral votes to win.

Now that it's a one-on-one fight, a candidate may change his or her approach to the voters. For one thing, the candidate now needs to appeal to all Americans, not just to those within his or her political party. A candidate's speeches and public appearances are designed to appeal to the broadest possible spectrum of American voters.

GETTING OUT THE VOTE

The political parties kick into high gear behind their candidate. During election years, political party members are active in nearly every city, town, and neighborhood in the United States

Volunteers go door-to-door in their neighborhood, trying to convince people to support their candidate on Election Day. They call people on the phone to gather support. They pass out leaflets, bumper stickers, and buttons with their candidate's name on them.

Party activists try to "get out the vote." Participation in presidential elections has been trending upward. In 2008, 56.8 percent of eligible voters cast a ballot, compared with 55.3 percent in 2004 and 51.3 percent in 2000.

All U.S. citizens over the age of 18 can vote if they have registered, or signed up to vote, and are not a felon. Everyone born in the United States and its territories is a citizen. People who immigrate to the United States may also vote if they become citizens first.

The political parties and other organizations, such as the League of Women Voters, try to convince all Americans to vote. They make it easy to register by setting up registration booths at stores, parks, and other public places. They give elderly or disabled people rides to voting places. They babysit for young children so that their parents can go to vote.

10

WHAT REALLY HAPPENS

on Election Day

A t last, Election Day arrives. The campaigning is over. The frenzy of activity, the speeches, the promises, and the television commercials have all stopped. Traditionally, candidates do not campaign on Election Day. They do what millions of other Americans do. They vote and then watch reports of the election on television.

AMERICANS GO TO THE POLLS

Every neighborhood or precinct has its own voting place, or poll. Usually, voting booths are set up in a public school, a firehouse, or the town hall. It is very likely that voting takes place in your school!

First, each voter must check in and prove he or she is registered to vote in that neighborhood. In some states, voters can register to vote right at the polling place on Election Day.

Traditionally, the voter goes into a space enclosed by a curtain. Inside is a machine to record the person's vote. That vote remains secret unless the voter tells someone.

If voters are away from home on Election Day, they can still cast a ballot. They have to get a special form, called an "absentee ballot," and mail it to the election office in their county.

In most elections, including the presidential elections, voters also choose people to fill more than one office. U.S. representatives run every two years, U.S. senators run every six years, and there may be a host of state and local candidates, plus issues such as permission to issue bonds.

In the 2004 Democratic primaries, Wisconsin experimented with allowing people to cast their votes through personal computers before Election Day. But no such plans were announced for the general election.

COUNTING UP THE VOTES

Local election officials at every voting place make sure things run smoothly and according to law. The officials are usually volunteers from both the Democratic and Republican parties. They record the votes counted by each voting machine and report them to a central election office. Officials from both parties are at the polling places to make sure that all votes are recorded and reported properly.

Some polling places have machines that punch a hole in a cardboard ballot card each time someone votes. At the end of Election Day, the officials take the cards to the central election office. Officials feed the cards into a computer that totals up the holes—votes—for each candidate, the same way a computer tallies up the answers. In 2000, Florida voters used a ballot that required punching out a hole beside the name of the desired candidate. That election was extremely close, and when the ballots were examined to recount them, it was discovered that the holes were confusing to voters, and many had not been punched all the way through. An incomplete punch was referred to as a "hanging chad."

Some kinds of voting machines tally votes mechanically. Voters push levers next to the name of the candidate they support. Inside the machine there is a counter for each candidate. It looks just like the mileage counter on a car's dashboard. When the election officials open the machine, they write down the number of votes for each candidate on an official form.

In recent years, many cities have tried to update their election equipment to use modern technology. However, these machines have had many problems. They are vulnerable to illegal tampering. Also, many electronic voting machines do not provide a printout, or paper trail, to make sure the voter's ballot was entered correctly. In the 2008 primaries, New Jersey was required to provide voters with a paper trail, but problems with its system delayed voting for hours. In South Carolina, eighty percent of the touch-screen machines didn't work properly. Some states have solved these problems with optical scanning, like the ones in supermarket checkout lines.

At each central election office, officials add up the votes from machines in their area. When officials at a state office add all the totals together, the winner of the election in that state is known!

PRIME-TIME RESULTS

The major television channels begin

reporting on the election early in the evening of Election Day. If you were thinking about watching your favorite show on this night, forget about it! All the major networks have their cameras turned on the most exciting show in the country: the presidential election.

As soon as possible, news organizations start collecting vote tallies from central election offices. They also conduct "exit polls." They ask voters leaving the polls who they voted for, and feed the results into a computer. Everyone wants to be first with the news. In 2000, the polls closed in eleven states by 7 P.M., Eastern Standard Time (EST). George W. Bush seemed to have an early lead. But at 8 P.M. the Voter News Service—working for ABC, NBC, CBS, CNN, Fox, and the AP—declared Al Gore the winner in Florida, and the news was announced. At 8:30 P.M., it appeared that Gore might win the presidency quickly, but Bush told reporters that he thought the networks had called the election too early. At 10:13 P.M., the Voter News Service took back its call in Florida. By 11 P.M., it appeared that the election was too close to call. All night long, the lead switched between candidates. By morning, it was clear that the election had been one of the closest in history, although several newspaper headlines proclaimed "Bush Wins!" It was thirty-six days before that news was official.

Afterward CNN hired a panel to report on the reporters. It scolded the networks for putting too much confidence in experts and polls. It said the Voter News Service used outdated technology. It suggested that the networks' practice of using key precincts to predict winners was not reliable. As a result, CNN said it would no longer use exit polls to call close races. It promised to fund a new precinct-sampling system.

PRIME-TIME ARGUMENTS

This was not the first time that the networks were accused of announcing a winner too soon. In 1980, long before people had finished voting, television reporters predicted that Ronald Reagan would beat President Jimmy Carter. Exit polls in the East showed Reagan a clear winner long before polls had closed in the West, where there is a three-hour time lag. Carter conceded at 9:45 P.M. (EST). The speech was aired in the West before the polls closed.

There were many candidates on the ballot besides those for president. These candidates in western states were mad. Once people knew that Reagan had won, many registered voters did not bother to go to the polls. Candidates charged that the early announcement unfairly affected the outcome of other races.

Surveys taken after the 1980 election showed that people all over the country were upset by early reporting. Congress held hearings on the issue. Some people suggested closing all the polls at the same time. Others said they should be open twenty-four hours on Election Day. Still others asked Congress to stop the networks from broadcasting early results. But news organizations claimed that the First Amendment right of a free press allows them to decide how to report information that they gather.

After the 2000 election, CNN agreed not to call winners when polls in some states are still open. Other networks may follow suit, but they are not legally bound to. Watch your favorite station in the upcoming election to see if the coverage improves.

THE LOSER AND THE WINNER SPEAK

Unless the election is close, one of the candidates usually admits defeat by 11 P.M., if not sooner. In each candidate's home state, hundreds of supporters have gathered in hotels. At this time, with the cameras rolling, the losing candidate gives a speech congratulating the winner and thanking supporters for all of their hard work. There is usually a lot of crying and booing in the audience. Shortly after, the winner appears in front of his or her party and gives a rousing speech to a cheering, jubilant crowd.

Now everyone knows who the next president will be, but there is one more hurdle to jump before the results are official. The votes of the people do not directly elect the president. The Electoral College does.

THE ELECTORAL COLLEGE

The Electoral College votes in mid-December. Each state gets as many electors in the Electoral College as it has senators and representatives in Congress. (How electors are chosen is up to the individual states.)

The electors meet at their state

capitals. They each write their choice for president on a paper ballot and put it in a locked box. On January 6, the president of the Senate counts the electoral votes in front of all the members of the House of Representatives and the Senate. A candidate needs a majority, or 270, electoral votes to win.

Electors are expected to vote for the candidate who got the most votes from the people of their state. It's a "winner-take-all" system. For example, California is a very big state and has fifty-five electors in the Electoral College. The candidate who wins the most votes from the people of California will get all fifty-five of California's electoral votes—even if the people's vote count was very close.

In very rare cases, electors voted for a candidate who did not win in their state. They are called "faithless electors." These electors cast their votes as a protest. They have never intended on or succeeded in changing the outcome of an election.

The Electoral College votes are counted without people taking much notice. Newspapers and television stations report the events in passing.

TIES AND THREE-WAY RACES

If no candidate gets a majority of the votes in the Electoral College, then the House of Representatives decides who the winner is. This can happen if there is a tie or if there are three candidates in the race and none of them gets more than half of the electoral vote. Each state can cast just one vote. To be elected president by the House, a candidate has to get 26 votes.

If no vice-presidential candidate gets a majority of votes in the Electoral College, then the Senate chooses between the two candidates with the most votes. In this case, each senator gets one vote.

Only two presidential elections have been decided by the House of Representatives. Thomas Jefferson won in the House in 1800, and John Quincy Adams in 1824.

ELECTORAL CONTROVERSIES

It is possible for a candidate to win the most votes from the people in the November election, but lose the race in the Electoral College! This can happen if the candidate loses in big electoral states by a very small number of votes, but wins in small electoral states by a very large number of votes.

In the 1800s, three candidates lost in the general election, but won the presidency after the Electoral College voted. In 1824, Andrew Jackson won the most votes in the general election, but the Electoral College chose John Quincy Adams for president. In 1876, Samuel Tilden won the general election, but some votes were questioned and there were charges of fraud. A special commission was set up to choose the president. After months of debate, the commission chose Tilden's opponent, Rutherford B. Hayes. In 1888, Grover Cleveland got the most popular votes, but Benjamin Harrison won in the Electoral College and became president.

The 2000 presidential election was very close. It took five weeks and a decision by the U.S. Supreme Court to determine the outcome. In the end, a recount of Florida ballots was stopped, and the state with its twenty-five electoral votes went to George W. Bush. Although Al Gore won the popular vote by 50,996,879 to 50,456,000, Bush won in the Electoral College, 271 to 266.

Today, some people think that the

Electoral College should be abolished. They think a direct election by the U.S. people would be more democratic. But changing the system would mean amending the Constitution, and such an amendment has never gotten enough support to become law.

THE NEW PRESIDENT

and the Next President

Almost immediately after the election is over, the losing party starts planning for next time. The search is on for a likely candidate. Presidential "wannabes" start putting out the word that they are interested in the job.

On January 20, the winner of the

presidential election stands before the Chief Justice of the United States and takes the Oath of Office. At that moment, the winner of the toughest race to run becomes president of the United States.

SELECTED ELECTION WEB SITES

Kids Talk Politics
http://www.kidstalkpolitics.com

Kids Voting USA
http://www.kidsvotingusa.org
Test your knowledge of the Constitution and share your wishes for our country with other kids.

The PBS Kids Democracy Project
http://www.pbs.org/democracy/kids
How does government affect me? What's it like to be president for a day? Register your vote about issues such as the environment and health care.

Scholastic.com

http://www.scholastic.com/teachers

Keep up with the latest election news reported by kids from all over the nation.

Young Politicians of America

http://www.ypa.org

Start your own political career at Young Politicians of America, devoted to learning about government through community service.

POLITICAL TALK:
A GLOSSARY OF TERMS

blog – a Web log or journal, posted on the Internet

blue states – states that tend to vote Democratic

conservative – traditionally, in the United States, someone who favors little government involvement in everyday life and limited government spending

consultant – a person paid to give advice to a campaign or a party

delegate – a person chosen to attend a political party convention

elector – a person chosen to represent a state's voters when the president is officially elected in January by the Electoral College

favorite son – a candidate nominated by a state that wants to honor him or her, but who has little chance of winning

Green Party – a party that was formed around concerns about the environment and corporate influence

liberal – traditionally, in the United States, someone who favors government involvement to further the rights of individuals and social justice, and who favors generous tax-supported spending

libertarian – a person who believes that the government's role in public life should be extremely limited and that individuals should be given maximum freedom

party chair – a person chosen to lead a political party at the local, state, or national level

plank – a statement about a party's position on a particular issue

platform – a party's set of goals and stances on major issues

Political Action Committee (PAC) – a group authorized to collect money to further its interests with political candidates

proportional voting – distributing a state's delegates by the proportional percentages that reflect the results of a primary rather than awarding all the power to the person who has the most votes

purple states – states with mixed support for Democrats and Republicans

negative ad – an advertisement that attacks another candidate rather than promoting the ideas and qualities of the candidate who pays for it

nominee – a person chosen by a political party to represent it in a general election

red states – states that tend to vote Republican

superdelegate – in the Democratic Party, a delegate who attends the convention because of a public office or political position he or she holds

swing state – a state that does not vote in favor of one party most of the time

trial balloon – an idea "floated" in the media to see what kind of reaction it will receive

winner-take-all voting – distributing all of a state's delegates to the person who gets the most votes rather than awarding them proportionally

PRESIDENTIAL ELECTION RESULTS

The following chart will show you who ran in each American presidential election. Until 1824, most electors were chosen by the state legislature—not the voters—so there are no popular vote totals for those years. The South Carolina legislature continued to pick its electors until 1860, when it seceded from the Union.

Use this key when referring to the following chart:

★   became president with the highest number of electoral votes

★★ became president when chosen by the House of Representatives

✓   became president through vice-presidential succession

✓✓ became president by Supreme Court ruling

Election Year	Candidates	Party	Popular Vote	Electoral Vote
1789	George Washington★	Federalist		69
	John Adams	Federalist		34
	Others	various		35
1792	George Washington★	Federalist		132
	John Adams	Federalist		77
	George Clinton	Anti-Federalist		50
	Others	various		5
1796	John Adams★	Federalist		71
	Thomas Jefferson	Democratic-Republican		68
	Thomas Pinckney	Federalist		5
	Aaron Burr	Democratic-Republican		30
	Others	various		48
1800	Thomas Jefferson★★	Democratic-Republican		73
	Aaron Burr	Democratic-Republican		73
	John Adams	Federalist		65
	Charles Pinckney	Federalist		64
	John Jay	Federalist		1
1804	Thomas Jefferson★	Democratic-Republican		162
	Charles Pinckney	Federalist		14
1808	James Madison★	Democratic-Republican		122
	Charles Pinckney	Federalist		47
	George Clinton	Democratic-Republican		6

Election Year	Candidates	Party	Popular Vote	Electoral Vote
1812	James Madison★	Democratic-Republican		128
	DeWitt Clinton	Federalist		89
1816	James Monroe★	Democratic-Republican		183
	Rufus King	Federalist		34
1820	James Monroe★	Democratic-Republican		231
	John Quincy Adams	Democratic-Republican		1
1824	John Quincy Adams★★	Democratic-Republican	108,740	84
	Andrew Jackson	Democratic-Republican	153,544	99
	William Crawford	Democratic-Republican	46,618	41
	Henry Clay	Democratic-Republican	47,136	37
1828	Andrew Jackson★	Democrat	647,286	178
	John Quincy Adams	Democratic-Republican	508,064	83
1832	Andrew Jackson★	Democrat	687,502	219
	Henry Clay	National Republican	530,189	49
	John Floyd	Independent	0	11
	William Wirt	Anti-Masonic	inconclusive	7

Election Year	Candidates	Party	Popular Vote	Electoral Vote
1836	Martin Van Buren★	Democrat	762,678	170
	William Henry Harrison	Whig		73
	Hugh White	Whig		26
	Daniel Webster	Whig		14
	Willie P. Mangum	Whig		11
		total Whig popular vote	735,561	
1840	William Henry Harrison★	Whig	1,275,016	234
	Martin Van Buren	Democrat	1,129,102	60
1841	John Tyler✓	Whig		
1844	James K. Polk★	Democrat	1,360,099	170
	James G. Birney	Liberty	62,300	0
1848	Zachary Taylor★	Whig	1,337,243	163
	Lewis Cass	Democrat	1,220,544	127
	Martin Van Buren	Free Soil	291,263	0
1850	Millard Fillmore✓	Whig		
1852	Franklin Pierce★	Democrat	1,601,274	254
	Winfield Scott	Whig	1,386,580	42
	John P. Hale	Free Soil	155,825	0
1856	James Buchanan★	Democrat	1,838,169	174
	John C. Fremont	Republican	1,341,264	114
	Millard Fillmore	American	874,534	8

Election Year	Candidates	Party	Popular Vote	Electoral Vote
1860	Abraham Lincoln★	Republican	1,866,452	180
	John C. Breckenridge	Democrat	847,953	72
	John Bell	Constitutional Union	590,631	39
	Stephen Douglas	Democrat	1,375,157	12
1864	Abraham Lincoln★	National Union	2,213,635	212
	George McClellan	Democrat	1,805,237	21
1865	Andrew Johnson✓	Democrat		
1868	Ulysses S. Grant★	Republican	3,012,833	214
	Horatio Seymour	Democrat	2,703,249	80
1872	Ulysses S. Grant★	Republican	3,597,132	286
	Horace Greeley	Democrat	2,834,079	died
	others	various	unknown	66
1876	Rutherford B. Hayes✓✓	Republican	4,036,298	185
	Samuel Tilden	Democrat	4,300,590	184
1880	James A. Garfield★	Republican	4,454,416	214
	Winfield Hancock	Democrat	4,444,952	155
	James B. Weaver	Greenback	308,578	0
1881	Chester A. Arthur✓	Republican		
1884	Grover Cleveland★	Democrat	4,874,986	219
	James G. Blaine	Republican	4,851,981	182
	Benjamin F. Butler	Greenback	175,370	0
	John P. St. John	Prohibition	150,369	0

Election Year	Candidates	Party	Popular Vote	Electoral Vote
1888	Benjamin Harrison★	Republican	5,447,129	233
	Grover Cleveland	Democrat	5,537,857	168
	Clinton B. Fisk	Prohibition	249,506	0
	Alson J. Streeter	Union Labor	146,935	0
1892	Grover Cleveland★	Democrat	5,556,918	277
	Benjamin Harrison	Republican	5,176,108	145
	James B. Weaver	People's Party	1,041,028	22
	John Bidwell	Prohibition	264,138	
1896	William McKinley★	Republican	7,104,779	271
	William J. Bryan	Democrat	6,502,925	176
1900	William McKinley★	Republican	7,207,923	292
	William J. Bryan	Democrat	6,358,138	155
	John G. Woolley	Prohibition	208,914	0
1901	Theodore Roosevelt✓	Republican		
1904	Theodore Roosevelt★	Republican	7,623,486	336
	Alton B. Parker	Democrat	5,077,911	140
	Eugene V. Debs	Socialist	420,793	0
	Silas Swallow	Prohibition	258,536	0
1908	William H. Taft★	Republican	7,678,908	321
	William J. Bryan	Democrat	6,409,104	162
	Eugene V. Debs	Socialist	420,793	0
	Eugene W. Chafin	Prohibition	253,840	0

Election Year	Candidates	Party	Popular Vote	Electoral Vote
1912	Woodrow Wilson★	Democrat	6,293,454	435
	Theodore Roosevelt	Progressive	4,119,538	88
	William H. Taft	Republican	3,484,980	8
	Eugene V. Debs	Socialist	900,672	0
	Eugene W. Chafin	Prohibition	206,275	0
1916	Woodrow Wilson★	Democrat	9,129,606	277
	Charles E. Hughes	Republican	8,538,221	254
	A. L. Benson	Socialist	585,113	0
	J. Frank Hanly	Prohibition	220,506	0
1920	Warren G. Harding★	Republican	16,152,200	404
	James M. Cox	Democrat	9,147,353	127
	Eugene V. Debs	Socialist	919,799	0
	P. P. Christenson	Farmer-Labor	265,411	0
1923	Calvin Coolidge✓	Republican		
1924	Calvin Coolidge★	Republican	15,725,016	382
	John W. Davis	Democrat	8,386,503	136
	Robert M. LaFollette	Progressive	4,822,856	13
1928	Herbert Hoover★	Republican	21,392,190	444
	Alfred E. Smith	Democrat	15,016,443	87
1932	Franklin D. Roosevelt★	Democrat	22,821,857	472
	Herbert Hoover	Republican	15,761,845	59
	Norman Thomas	Socialist	881,951	0
1936	Franklin D. Roosevelt★	Democrat	27,476,673	523
	Alfred M. Landon	Republican	16,679,583	8
	William Lemke	Union	892,793	0

Election Year	Candidates	Party	Popular Vote	Electoral Vote
1940	Franklin D. Roosevelt★	Democrat	27,243,466	449
	Wendell Willkie	Republican	22,304,755	82
1944	Franklin D. Roosevelt★	Democrat	25,602,505	432
	Thomas Dewey	Republican	22,006,278	99
1945	Harry S. Truman✓	Democrat		
1948	Harry S. Truman★	Democrat	24,105,695	303
	Thomas Dewey	Republican	21,969,170	189
	Strom Thurmond	States' Rights	1,169,021	39
	Henry Wallace	Progressive	1,158,103	0
1952	Dwight D. Eisenhower★	Republican	33,778,963	442
	Adlai Stevenson	Democrat	27,314,992	89
1956	Dwight D. Eisenhower★	Republican	35,227,096	303
	Adlai Stevenson	Democrat	25,738,765	73
1960	John F. Kennedy★	Democrat	34,227,096	303
	Richard M. Nixon	Republican	34,107,646	219
1963	Lyndon B. Johnson✓	Democrat		
1964	Lyndon B. Johnson★	Democrat	42,826,463	486
	Barry Goldwater	Republican	27,175,770	52
1968	Richard M. Nixon★	Republican	31,710,470	301
	Hubert H. Humphrey	Democrat	30,898,055	191
	George C. Wallace	American Independent	9,446,167	46

Election Year	Candidates	Party	Popular Vote	Electoral Vote
1972	Richard M. Nixon★	Republican	46,740,323	520
	George McGovern	Democrat	28,901,598	17
1974	Gerald Ford✓	Republican		
1976	Jimmy Carter★	Democrat	40,830,753	297
	Gerald Ford	Republican	39,147,793	240
1980	Ronald Reagan★	Republican	43,901,812	489
	Jimmy Carter	Democrat	35,483,820	49
	John Anderson	Independent	5,719,722	0
1984	Ronald Reagan★	Republican	54,451,531	525
	Walter Mondale	Democrat	37,565,334	13
1988	George H. W. Bush★	Republican	48,881,278	426
	Michael Dukakis	Democrat	41,805,374	111
1992	William J. Clinton★	Democrat	44,908,254	370
	George H. W. Bush	Republican	39,102,343	168
	H. Ross Perot	Independent	19,741,065	0
1996	William J. Clinton★	Democrat	45,628,667	379
	Robert Dole	Republican	37,869,435	159
	H. Ross Perot	Reform	7,874,283	0
2000	George W. Bush★	Republican	50,456,002	271
	Albert Gore	Democrat	50,999,897	266
	Ralph Nader	Green	2,882,955	0
2004	George W. Bush★	Republican	62,028,285	286
	John Kerry	Democrat	59,028,109	251

Election Year	Candidates	Party	Popular Vote	Electoral Vote
2008	Barack Obama★	Democrat	66,882,230	365
	John McCain	Republican	58,343,671	173

GEORGE WASHINGTON

BORN: Feb. 22, 1732
BIRTHPLACE: Westmoreland Co., VA
DIED: Dec. 14, 1799
DATES OF TERMS:
April 30, 1789–March 3, 1793;
March 4, 1793–March 3, 1797
PARTY: Federalist

JOHN ADAMS

BORN: Oct. 30, 1735
BIRTHPLACE: Braintree, MA
DIED: July 4, 1826
DATES OF TERM:
March 4, 1797–March 3, 1801
PARTY: Federalist

THOMAS JEFFERSON

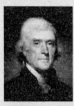

BORN: April 13, 1743
BIRTHPLACE: Shadwell, VA
DIED: July 4, 1826
DATES OF TERMS:
March 4, 1801–March 3, 1805;
March 4, 1805–March 3, 1809
PARTY: Democratic-Republican

JAMES MADISON

BORN: March 16, 1751
BIRTHPLACE: Port Conway, VA
DIED: June 28, 1836
DATES OF TERMS:
March 4, 1809–March 3, 1813;
March 4, 1813–March 3, 1817
PARTY: Democratic-Republican

JAMES MONROE

BORN: April 28, 1758
BIRTHPLACE: Westmoreland Co., VA
DIED: July 4, 1831
DATES OF TERMS:
March 4, 1817–March 3, 1821;
March 4, 1821–March 3, 1825
PARTY: Democratic-Republican

JOHN QUINCY ADAMS

BORN: July 11, 1767
BIRTHPLACE: Braintree, MA
DIED: Feb. 23, 1848
DATES OF TERM:
March 4, 1825–March 3, 1829
PARTY: Democratic-Republican

ANDREW JACKSON

BORN: March 15, 1767
BIRTHPLACE: Waxhaw, SC
DIED: June 8, 1845
DATES OF TERMS:
March 4, 1829–March 3, 1833;
March 4, 1833–March 3, 1837
PARTY: Democrat

MARTIN VAN BUREN

BORN: Dec. 5, 1782
BIRTHPLACE: Kinderhook, NY
DIED: July 24, 1862
DATES OF TERM:
March 4, 1837–March 3, 1841
PARTY: Democrat

WILLIAM HENRY HARRISON

BORN: Feb. 9, 1773
BIRTHPLACE: Berkeley, VA
DIED: April 4, 1841
DATES OF TERM:
March 4, 1841–April 4, 1841*
PARTY: Whig

JOHN TYLER

BORN: March 29, 1790
BIRTHPLACE: Greenway, VA
DIED: Jan. 18, 1862
DATES OF TERM:
April 6, 1841–March 3, 1845
PARTY: Whig

JAMES K. POLK

BORN: Nov. 2, 1795
BIRTHPLACE: Mecklenburg Co., NC
DIED: June 15, 1849
DATES OF TERM:
March 4, 1845–March 3, 1849
PARTY: Democrat

ZACHARY TAYLOR

BORN: Nov. 24, 1784
BIRTHPLACE: Orange Co., VA
DIED: July 9, 1850
DATES OF TERM:
March 4, 1849–July 9, 1850*
PARTY: Whig

MILLARD FILLMORE

BORN: Jan. 7, 1800
BIRTHPLACE: Locke, NY
DIED: March 8, 1874
DATES OF TERM:
July 10, 1850–March 3, 1853
PARTY: Whig

JAMES BUCHANAN

BORN: April 23, 1791
BIRTHPLACE: Mercersburg, PA
DIED: June 1, 1868
DATES OF TERM:
March 4, 1857–March 3, 1861
PARTY: Democratic

ANDREW JOHNSON

BORN: Dec. 29, 1808
BIRTHPLACE: Raleigh, NC
DIED: July 31, 1875
DATES OF TERM:
April 15, 1865–March 3, 1869
PARTY: Democrat

FRANKLIN PIERCE

BORN: Nov. 23, 1804
BIRTHPLACE: Hillsborough, NH
DIED: Oct. 8, 1869
DATES OF TERM:
March 4, 1853–March 3, 1857
PARTY: Democrat

ABRAHAM LINCOLN

BORN: Feb. 12, 1809
BIRTHPLACE: Hardin Co., KY
DIED: April 15, 1865
DATES OF TERMS:
March 4, 1861–March 3, 1865;
March 4, 1865–April 15, 1865*
PARTY: Republican

ULYSSES S. GRANT

BORN: April 27, 1822
BIRTHPLACE: Point Pleasant, OH
DIED: July 23, 1885
DATES OF TERMS:
March 4, 1869–March 3, 1873;
March 4, 1873–March 3, 1877
PARTY: Republican

RUTHERFORD B. HAYES

BORN: Oct. 4, 1822
BIRTHPLACE: Delaware, OH
DIED: Jan. 17, 1893
DATES OF TERM:
March 4, 1877–March 3, 1881
PARTY: Republican

CHESTER A. ARTHUR

BORN: Oct. 5, 1829
BIRTHPLACE: Fairfield, VT
DIED: Nov. 18, 1886
DATES OF TERM:
Sept. 20, 1881–March 3, 1885
PARTY: Republican

BENJAMIN HARRISON

BORN: Aug. 20, 1833
BIRTHPLACE: North Bend, OH
DIED: March 13, 1901
DATES OF TERM:
March 4, 1889–March 3, 1893
PARTY: Republican

JAMES A. GARFIELD

BORN: Nov. 19, 1831
BIRTHPLACE: Orange, OH
DIED: Sept. 19, 1881
DATES OF TERM:
March 4, 1881–Sept. 19, 1881*
PARTY: Republican

GROVER CLEVELAND

BORN: March 18, 1837
BIRTHPLACE: Caldwell, NJ
DIED: June 24, 1908
DATES OF TERM:
March 4, 1885–March 3, 1889
PARTY: Democrat

GROVER CLEVELAND

BORN: March 18, 1837
BIRTHPLACE: Caldwell, NJ
DIED: June 24, 1908
DATES OF TERM:
March 4, 1893–
March 3, 1897**
PARTY: Democrat

WILLIAM MCKINLEY

BORN: Jan. 29, 1843
BIRTHPLACE: Niles, OH
DIED: Sept. 14, 1901
DATES OF TERMS:
March 4, 1897–March 3, 1901;
March 4, 1901–Sept. 14, 1901*
PARTY: Republican

THEODORE ROOSEVELT

BORN: Oct. 27, 1858
BIRTHPLACE: New York, NY
DIED: Jan. 6, 1919
DATES OF TERMS:
Sept. 14, 1901–March 3, 1905;
March 4, 1905–March 3, 1909
PARTY: Republican

WILLIAM H. TAFT

BORN: Sept. 15, 1857
BIRTHPLACE: Cincinnati, OH
DIED: March 8, 1930
DATES OF TERM:
March 4, 1909–March 3, 1913
PARTY: Republican

WOODROW WILSON

BORN: Dec. 28, 1856
BIRTHPLACE: Staunton, VA
DIED: Feb. 3, 1924
DATES OF TERMS:
March 4, 1913–March 3, 1917;
March 4, 1917–March 3, 1921
PARTY: Democrat

WARREN G. HARDING

BORN: Nov. 2, 1865
BIRTHPLACE: Corsica, OH
DIED: Aug. 2, 1923
DATES OF TERM:
March 4, 1921–Aug. 2, 1923*
PARTY: Republican

CALVIN COOLIDGE

BORN: July 4, 1872
BIRTHPLACE: Plymouth Notch, VT
DIED: Jan. 5, 1933
DATES OF TERMS:
Aug. 3, 1923–March 3, 1925;
March 4, 1925–March 3, 1929
PARTY: Republican

HERBERT C. HOOVER

BORN: Aug. 10, 1874
BIRTHPLACE: West Branch, IA
DIED: Oct. 20, 1964
DATES OF TERM:
March 4, 1929–March 3, 1933
PARTY: Republican

HARRY S. TRUMAN

BORN: May 8, 1884
BIRTHPLACE: Lamar, MO
DIED: Dec. 26, 1972
DATES OF TERMS:
April 12, 1945–Jan. 20, 1949;
Jan. 20, 1949–Jan. 20, 1953
PARTY: Democrat

JOHN F. KENNEDY

BORN: May 29, 1917
BIRTHPLACE: Brookline, MA
DIED: Nov. 22, 1963
DATES OF TERM:
Jan. 20, 1961–Nov. 22, 1963*
PARTY: Democrat

FRANKLIN D. ROOSEVELT

BORN: Jan. 30, 1882
BIRTHPLACE: Hyde Park, NY
DIED: April 12, 1945
DATES OF TERMS:
March 4, 1933–Jan. 19, 1937;
Jan. 20, 1937–Jan. 19, 1941;
Jan. 20, 1941–Jan. 19, 1945;
Jan. 20, 1945–April 12, 1945*
PARTY: Democrat

DWIGHT D. EISENHOWER

BORN: Oct. 14, 1890
BIRTHPLACE: Denison, TX
DIED: March 28, 1969
DATES OF TERMS:
Jan. 20, 1953–Jan. 20, 1957;
Jan. 20, 1957–Jan. 20, 1961
PARTY: Republican

LYNDON B. JOHNSON

BORN: Aug. 27, 1908
BIRTHPLACE: Stonewall, TX
DIED: Jan. 22, 1973
DATES OF TERMS:
Nov. 22, 1963–Jan. 20, 1965;
Jan. 20, 1965–Jan. 20, 1969
PARTY: Democrat

RICHARD M. NIXON

BORN: Jan. 9, 1913
BIRTHPLACE: Yorba Linda, CA
DIED: April 22, 1994
DATES OF TERMS:
Jan. 20, 1969–Jan. 20, 1973;
Jan. 20, 1973–Aug. 9, 1974***
PARTY: Republican

JIMMY CARTER

BORN: Oct. 1, 1924
BIRTHPLACE: Plains, GA
DIED:
DATES OF TERM:
Jan. 20, 1977–Jan. 20, 1981
PARTY: Democrat

GEORGE H. W. BUSH

BORN: June 12, 1924
BIRTHPLACE: Milton, MA
DIED:
DATES OF TERM:
Jan. 20, 1989–Jan. 20, 1993
PARTY: Republican

GERALD FORD

BORN: July 14, 1913
BIRTHPLACE: Omaha, NE
DIED: Dec. 26, 2006
DATES OF TERM:
Aug. 9, 1974–Jan. 20, 1977
PARTY: Republican

RONALD REAGAN

BORN: Feb. 6, 1911
BIRTHPLACE: Tampico, IL
DIED: June 5, 2004
DATES OF TERMS:
Jan 20, 1981–Jan. 20, 1985;
Jan. 20, 1985–Jan. 20, 1989
PARTY: Republican

WILLIAM J. CLINTON

BORN: Aug. 19, 1946
BIRTHPLACE: Hope, AR
DIED:
DATES OF TERMS:
Jan. 20, 1993–Jan. 20, 1997;
Jan. 20, 1997–Jan. 20, 2001
PARTY: Democrat

GEORGE W. BUSH

BORN: July 6, 1946
BIRTHPLACE: New Haven, CT
DIED:
DATES OF TERMS:
Jan. 20, 2001–Jan. 20, 2005;
Jan. 20, 2005–Jan. 20, 2009
PARTY: Republican

BARACK OBAMA

BORN: Aug. 4, 1961
BIRTHPLACE: Honolulu, HI
DIED:
DATES OF TERM:
Jan. 20, 2009–
PARTY: Democrat

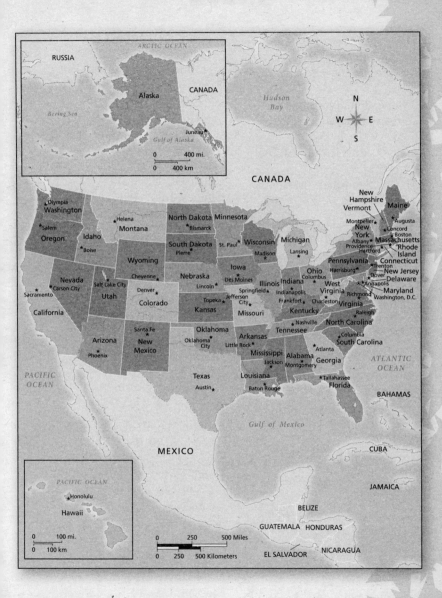

RUSSIA

ARCTIC OCEAN

Alaska

CANADA

Hudson
Bay

Bering Sea

Gulf of Alaska

Juneau

| 0 | 400 mi. |
| 0 | 400 km |

N
W E
S

CANADA

New
Hampshire
Vermont   Maine

Montpelier   ★Augusta
New   ★Concord
York   ★Boston
Albany★ ★★Massachusetts
Providence★ ★★Rhode
Hartford   Island
Connecticut
New Jersey
Trenton★
Dover★ Delaware
Annapolis★ Maryland
Washington, D.C.

Olympia★
Washington
Helena★
Salem★   Montana
Oregon   Idaho
Boise★

North Dakota   Minnesota
Bismarck★
South Dakota St. Paul★ Wisconsin Michigan
Pierre★   Madison★ Lansing★

Ohio
Columbus★
Pennsylvania
Harrisburg★

Wyoming
Cheyenne★

Nevada
Carson City★
Salt Lake City★
Sacramento★
California

Utah

Denver★
Colorado

Nebraska
Lincoln★

Iowa
Des Moines★

Illinois Indiana
Springfield★ Indianapolis★
Jefferson Frankfort★
City★   Kentucky

West
Virginia
Charleston★
Richmond★
Virginia
Raleigh★
North Carolina

Topeka★
Kansas   Missouri

Nashville★

Arizona
Phoenix★

Santa Fe★
New
Mexico

Oklahoma
Oklahoma★
City

Arkansas
Little Rock★

Tennessee

Columbia★
South Carolina

Mississippi Alabama
Jackson★ Montgomery★

Atlanta★
Georgia

Texas
Austin★

Louisiana
Baton Rouge★

Tallahassee★
Florida

ATLANTIC
OCEAN

BAHAMAS

PACIFIC
OCEAN

Gulf of Mexico

MEXICO

CUBA

JAMAICA

PACIFIC OCEAN

Honolulu★
Hawaii

BELIZE

GUATEMALA HONDURAS

EL SALVADOR NICARAGUA

| 0 | 100 mi. |
| 0 | 100 km |

| 0 | 250 | 500 Miles |
| 0 | 250 | 500 Kilometers |

INDEX